OBSERVE THE RUSTLING LEAVES

James O'Halloran SDB

Observe the Rustling Leaves

THE CHURCH AND WORLD OF THE FUTURE

the columba press

First published in 2007 by
the columba press
55A Spruce Avenue, Stillorgan Industrial Park,
Blackrock, Co Dublin

Cover designed by Bill Bolger
Cover picture and illustrations by
Christine Crotty
Origination by The Columba Press
Printed in Ireland by ColourBooks Ltd, Dublin

ISBN 978-1-85607-576-3

Acknowledgements
Thanks to Emer Ryan, Sr Jenny Perkins FMA, Leo
Malone and Steve Harris for help with this book.

For Callan and its people
(past, present and to come),
especially those from whom I learned
the value of family, friendship and community.

The Father laughs with the Son;
The Son laughs with the Father.
The Father likes the Son;
The Son likes the Father.
The Father delights in the Son;
The Son delights in the Father.
The Father loves the Son;
The Son loves the Father.
The laughter, liking, delighting,
loving is the Holy Spirit.
(Meister Eckhart)

Preface

This year, 2007, my native town of Callan, Co Kilkenny, Ireland, celebrates the 8th centenary of its foundation. As part of this celebration, I have been asked to give an address on the subject of 'The Church and World of the Future'. Needless to say, I feel deeply honoured by this invitation. Being recognised by your native town carries a satisfaction that no other honour can bestow. I now understand what they mean when Kilkenny hurlers, such as Henry Sheflin, D. J. Carey and John Power, say that winning the Kilkenny County Championship for their club is sweeter than even winning the All Ireland Final!

I find the subject on which I was asked to speak intriguing; it's the universality of it that fascinates. Had I been asked to give a talk entitled 'A Window on Callan of the 1940s', for example, it would not have been unexpected – my vivid memories of the town and its people are of that period. I would have found myself talking about the greatest raconteur I ever met, Dick Kelly Snr of Mill Street, and of places like the Turning Hole, Butler's Grove and James's

Well. The remainder of my life has been spent largely in faraway lands. But, no doubt, bearing in mind my own life experience and the interpenetration of the universal and the local, the organisers of the events to mark the centenary wisely chose the subject 'The Church and World of the Future'.

But, then, Callan has always been keenly aware of the world beyond its confines. How could it be otherwise, since in search of a livlihood so many of its sons and daughters, as part of a virtual Irish exodus, took the emigrant ship to America, Canada, Australia, Britain and many other lands. I recall meeting a McBride in a town bordering the jungle in Ecuador. He spoke no English, pronounced his name 'Macbreeday', as in Spanish, and knew only vaguely that his forebears had come from somewhere far beyond the seas.

Outstanding people
The town has also produced people of renown who have made an impact both nationally and internationally. In this context, among so many others, we could mention: famed Benedictine Abbess Mary Butler, Blessed Edmund Ignatius Rice (founder of the Irish Christian Brothers), architect James Hoban, diarist Humphrey

O'Sullivan, Father Tom O'Shea (co-founder of the Callan Tenant Protection Society), poet John Locke, historian and patriot Thomas Shelley, artist Tony O'Malley and dramatist Thomas Kilroy.

The contribution of Brother Rice to education in Ireland and around the world has been enormous. Without it, many an Irish child would have had little or no education at all, and the same would undoubtedly be true of young people elsewhere. He was a person well ahead of his times. Already in the 1800s, for example, he opposed the use of corporal punishment in schools.

James Hoban was of course the architect of the White House in Washington DC. In 1996, I was taken on a tour of the White House by President Clinton's Advance Press Secretary, Ann Edwards. This through the good offices of Adrian O'Neill of the Irish Embassy, a friend of mine for many years. When I told Ann that I came from the same parish as the architect of 'this venerable pile', she got quite excited, and for a few exquisite moments I basked in the reflected glory of James Hoban. Ann mentioned that some days earlier a group of English officials were given the same tour as ourselves and were told that in 1814 the White

House was damaged by fire. I wondered if their guide did this with tongue in cheek because the arsonists were none other than – British troops!

Humphrey O'Sullivan's diary is unique insofar as it is a sustained account of the lives of ordinary people in a small provincial town during the years 1827–35; it was also written in Irish, widely spoken in the West Kilkenny area at the time. Kerry people proudly point out that O'Sullivan was born near Killarney in 1780. True. But Humphrey spent practically all his life in Callan and is an adopted Callan man, so to all Kerry people we say: 'Hands off!'

Fr Tom O'Shea's importance is emphasised in *Callan County Kilkenny: A Short Guide to its History, Monuments and People* (Callan Heritage Society). In this volume, Joseph Kennedy writes:

> The 'Callan Tenant Protection Society' which was founded in the Town Hall on the 14th of October 1849, was to evolve into one of the most important movements in Irish history, the 'Irish Tenant League'. This organisation was the forerunner of the famous Land League of the 1880s, which finally ended 'Landlordism' in Ireland. It was founded by the 'Callan Curates' Father

Matt O'Keefe from Higginstown, Clara, and Father Tom O'Shea from Cappahayden, near Callan.[1]

Callan's beloved

Poet John Locke (1847–89) is undoubtedly the town's darling, though his achievements would hardly match those of some of the fore-going. That the Callan hurling team is named the John Lockes and their local pitch John Locke Park are precise indicators of his popul-arity. In Kilkenny, only achieving eternal salv-ation is – possibly – more important than win-ning the All Ireland Hurling Final. So what was the secret of the adulation for Locke? A variety of factors, I would suggest. As a scholar at the Callan National School, grandly known as the Academy, he was regarded as the most stylish hurler that had been seen there for a long time. More seriously, again with the proviso that there can be anything more serious than the national game, the sweet nostalgia of his poetry spoke to the hearts of people. How many child-ren, not only from Callan but from Ireland and elsewhere, rejoiced in and committed to memory

1. Kennedy, Joseph, *Callan County Kilkenny: A Short Guide to its History, Monuments and People*, Callan: Callan Heritage Society, 2000, p 21.

his anthem for the returning exile in 'Dawn on the Irish Coast':

> T'anam chun Dia! but there it is –
> The dawn on the hills of Ireland!
> God's angels lifting the night's black veil
> From the fair, sweet face of my sireland!
> O, Ireland! isn't it grand you look –
> Like a bride in her rich adornin'!
> With all the pent-up love of my heart
> I bid you the top of the mornin'!

John Locke had a special love for the King's River, the stream that gently wends its way through Callan. It's a love that I share with him. As a boy I had a romance with that river. Spent hours and hours on its banks, watching the long-haired weeds swaying gently in the murmuring waters, imagining a mysterious world below the undulating weeds and darting silver trout. In that place I dreamed dreams and had what a bard evocatively called 'my long, long thoughts'. So my own favourite poem of Locke is 'The Calm Avonree' (another anglicised form of the Gaelic *Abhainn Rí*, King's River):

> Ah me! I could fly, like a bird o'er the ocean,
> To the home of my heart, to the land of my love,

I'd be up on the wings, with an exile's devo-
tion;
And dare every danger the dark seas above;
Again would I roam, through the green
shady bowers,
Where the boys used to drill e'er I first
crossed the sea,
And I'd weave for my Kathleen a garland of
flowers,
On the green mossy banks of the calm
Avonree.

In this verse we also have the key to John
Locke's destiny. Because of his involvement in
the Fenian movement, he found himself in
Kilkenny gaol at the tender age of twenty. On
being released, he was continually harassed
and eventually went into reluctant exile, first of
all to Manchester and then to New York in
1867. There he settled down as a journalist in
the Irish milieu and married Mary Cooney, a
native of Kilkenny City. His marriage was
happy but, sadly, short. He died in 1889 at the
age of forty-one.

The elements that contributed to John
Locke's iconic status, therefore, were: his being
a superb hurler, a poet of the heart, a patriot
who suffered for his country (whereas we Irish

tend to trim tall poppies, we are genuinely full of compassion for the victim of persecution or whatever), and he died young. That he possessed fair curly hair and a captivating smile must have endeared him to people as well, especially to the ladies. My grandmother Maggie O'Reilly, in her time a striking beauty, was the first to tell me about John Locke. She would have been born just after he left Callan, yet his memory remained vivid in the town. She also mentioned a sister of his, Ellen Locke, whom she seemed to have known fairly well. Ellen lived at the top of Bridge Street where the post office was at the time.

Above all, John Locke was a good person and devout Christian. But maybe we should leave the last word on the man to his wife Mary, herself no mean poet:

God gave me all I asked in life,
Companion equal in the strife,
In all my thoughts to share;
A husband, high-souled, noble-browed,
Of whom a princess might be proud,
A man of talents rare.

Scholar of substance
Of the outstanding Callan people mentioned so far, the only ones I saw in the flesh were artist

Tony O'Malley and dramatist Thomas Kilroy.
Tony O'Malley I saw, yet never had the privilege of speaking to, a fact I regret. His brother
Mattie and sister Rita – lovely people – I knew
well through frequent visits to their quaint little
sweet shop in lower Bridge Street. Mattie
would sometimes meet you with a few accur-
ately, but gently, delivered punches to the jaw
and rib cage (he was quite a boxer).

I was actually in the same school as Thomas
Kilroy for about two years, but have no clear
memories of him there. I can never remember
speaking to him either. I do, however, have one
clear vignette of Tommy, as he was called. He
was going home from school and it was his
school bag that first caught my attention. It was
unusually laden with books. I then paid attention to the flaming red-haired bearer. The glasses
had slid down his nose in professorial fashion
and he pushed them back up. If I had known
the word *nerd* at the time, it would have fitted
perfectly. I vaguely recall a hurley stick as well,
but that would only have been for political cor-
rectness. Everyone in Kilkenny was expected to
carry a hurley – you'd never know when you
might be called up! Even at that young age my
deep impression was that here was a serious
intellectual. From his plays I have verified that

my original diagnosis was correct. One of my most pleasing dramatic experiences was attending his Irish adaptation of Chekov's *Seagull* in London's West End, featuring Vanessa Redgrave and Terence Stamp. In it there was this character who kept on repeating some telling remark he had made *ad nauseam*, and I really had to laugh, because I'd so often met 'characters' around Callan who had a habit of doing just that.

I also enjoyed his prize winning novel *The Big Chapel* and often got into an argument with a Callan person about it. Time and again, when the historicity of some detail would be questioned, I found myself protesting: 'Hey, the novel is historical, not history. It's fiction!'

One other thing I found I had in common with Thomas Kilroy was a deep admiration for the American author Flannery O'Connor. As a writer I found her so different, quite unique. In the posthumous publication of her letters in the *Habit of Being*, I was pleasantly surprised to discover that Thomas paid her a visit at her home in Milledgeville, Georgia, where she struggled to write – while slowly losing her battle to lupus disease. She died at thirty-nine.

Callan and the church and world

Mention of Brother Rice, Fr Tom O'Shea and an exemplary Christian layman like John Locke reminds us of Callan's relationship with, and outstanding contribution to, the church. I later saw their likes in Latin America of the 1970s. Archbishop Romero, who gave his life in the cause of justice, would be an example. However, it wasn't only Callan figures such as Rice, O'Shea and Locke, who served their church and world well. Countless missionaries (priests, religious and lay) and ordinary emigrants of deep faith from the town did the same. I would like to pay tribute to them all here. I am convinced that, when we 'shuffle off this mortal coil', we will find that many of the greatest saints in heaven will have passed their lives on earth in relative obscurity. Their names may not be written in the annals of history, but they will loom largely where it matters most – in the Book of Life.

Nor were the lives of Callan people, historically, without suffering. They were often ravaged by oppression, poverty, famine and disease. If the walls of the Workhouse could talk, what stories they would have to tell. The Great Hunger of the 1840s was particularly traumatic. It burned into the psyche of people. My grand-

mother, Maggie O'Reilly, served in the Workhouse Hospital as a young woman. Having
been born in 1870, she would have known, and
listened to, the stories of people who were
scarred by the Famine. She told me how vic-
tims were found dead with their mouths still
stained by the grass they had been eating to
assuage their raging hunger. She talked also of
overladen carts taking people for sad burial in
the graveyard at Cherryfield. We Callan people
must be eternally grateful to Afri for erecting a
fit monument in Cherryfield to all those name-
less people who were, after all, our forebears. If
I might add a personal note, I am proud that
the founder of Afri, Fr Sean McFerran, was like
myself a Salesian of Don Bosco, and that I had
the honour of serving for a time on the Afri
executive.

And spare a special thought for the trials of
our emigrants who, down the years, were
forced to leave their homeland with heavy
hearts, often with no prospect of ever returning. The haunting song 'She lived beside the
Anner' captures the plight of them all for me in
a couple of heart-rending lines:

O brave brave Irish girls, we well may call
you brave,
For the least of all your perils is the stormy
ocean wave …
(Charles Joseph Kickham)

The people of Callan also suffered greatly
through divisions resulting from the parish
Schism (1869–81). The main protagonists in the
strife were Fr Robert O'Keefe, parish priest of
the town and the Bishop of Ossory, Dr Edward
Walsh. The sad episode, which resonated in the
halls of the Vatican and chambers of the British
Parliament, trailed bitter consequences for
decades and inspired two outstanding novels
(*The Greatest of These*, by Francis McManus and,
as already noted, *The Big Chapel*, by Thomas
Kilroy). Patrick Hogan, now deceased and a
close friend of mine since we were altar boys in
the Friary together in the 1940s, produced a
fine historical study of the Schism entitled 'The
Fr Robert O'Keefe Controversy 1869-81'
(*Kilkenny History and Society*, 1990). One
intriguing aspect of the whole affair was the
passion with which the populace approached
matters religious; such passion may now seem
strange to us in times that are more secular and
apathetic.

To underline the devotion with which parishioners lined up on one or other side of the controversy in the Schism, an experience of my maternal grandfather, James O'Reilly, is illuminating. I distinctly remember him telling me in hushed tones of having gone, as an eleven-year-old, to the funeral of Fr O'Keefe. The rain on that day seems to have been on a scale that would have surprised even Noah. James, however, braved the elements and went to the burial in bare feet. Whether this was because of poverty or the appalling weather, I do not know. Going barefoot may in the conditions prevailing have proved the more practical option, yet I somehow got the impression that the fact was given as evidence of the awesome tumult in the heavens at the passing of Fr O'Keefe.

* * *

In conclusion, I believe the foregoing has helped us to realise that the world is the little town and the little town the world. We see the local dramas of Callan (religious, social, political, artistic, cultural, economic and so forth) played out on all continents. We continually respond practically to re-runs of our travails of famine, disease, exile and religious strife coming from all parts of the planet. We have seen too our alertness to world issues through the Irish abroad. Given these realities, it is entirely appropriate that I was requested to give the address that follows on 'The Church and World of the Future'. Its fundamental theme is community. Putting closure to any divisions we may have had in the past and ridding ourselves of the petty snobbery that has so often bred personal and public tragedy in our town and country, may it help us face the future with a united front. If we recall the perceptive observation of Cavafy, this heartfelt appeal is also relevant to those of our people who now dwell far from the calm Avonree. These are his poignant words: 'In those few fields or streets of your childhood, no matter where you roam, you will live – and so also will you die.' In a sense, we never leave Callan.

The Church and World of the Future

They say that if you want to give the Almighty a laugh, you should just tell the Lord your future plans. So to speculate on the church and world of the future is a daunting task: a nuclear war next week could render the whole project academic.

From our human perspective there are two futures – the future known only to God and the future as we visualise it. We plan ahead for Christmas because usually it arrives without fail on the 25 December each year. If it could decide arbitrarily to pop up on 1 January, we would be completely flummoxed.

My thoughts on the future church and world are, of course, based on the signs of the times in the present. If we want to see in what direction the winds of change are blowing, we must look to the rustle of leaves now. I have taken the title 'The Church and World of the Future' for this presentation. Originally, it was merely 'The Church of the Future', but as I went along I came to a point where I said: 'Hey! The church is *in* the world. Their destinies are tied together.' What's good for the church of the future, has to be good for the world of the future. So starting from a church point of view, I also try to see the implications for the world. Since all life is a story, I begin with a story.

Sylvia's story
In March 1994 (the last millennium!) I facilitated a workshop on small Christian community in Nairobi. At the beginning the participants were sharing experiences of such communities and I found particularly interesting the anecdote of a young woman called Sylvia. 'When I left school,' she informed us, 'I would say I had the faith. I lived on the outskirts of Nairobi and every Sunday travelled by bus to the centre of the city where I attended Mass at the Holy Family Basilica. But the basilica was very big and I didn't know anyone much. I felt alone. In the pulpit, the priest talked of love and community, yet somehow I didn't understand. Then going home one Sunday and feeling a bit depressed, I said to myself, "I don't have a spiritual friend in the whole world." '

This was the low point of Sylvia's narrative and what she was saying was truly sad, because none of us goes to heaven alone. We are saved through relationships. The Bible says it is not good for us to be alone (cf Genesis 2:8).

Persons who cut themselves off from others are a human contradiction because, without one another, we could not even learn to be persons. Without the sunshine of love and the rain of acceptance, we could not grow as persons. We couldn't talk, maybe not even walk.

Sylvia went on to say, however: 'Soon afterwards I came across a small Christian community in my area and became a member. With that everything changed. In the community I didn't simply *hear* about love, as in the basilica; I actually experienced it, tasted the sweetness of togetherness. And little by little, I grew spiritually, gained new ideas, made good friends and was able to take part in work for my neighbourhood. I blossomed as a person. No longer am I the girl who travelled alone into Nairobi, was lost in the big church and returned home downcast.'

Community like the Trinity
What Sylvia was experiencing by the power of the Holy Spirit, people are experiencing in thousands of such groups on every continent. This we recognised and affirmed at the Third International Consultation on Small Christian Communities held in Cochabamba, Bolivia, in 1999. I myself had the privilege of taking part

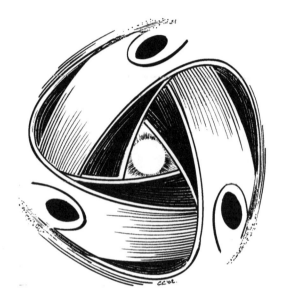

in that enlightening assembly, as co-ordinator of an ecumenical European team. Furthermore, the Spirit, already at work at the grassroots, blew strongly on this theme at the Second Vatican Council. Paragraph 4 in the *Dogmatic Constitution on the Church (Lumen Gentium)* says:

> the universal Church is seen to be "a people brought into unity from the union of the Father, Son and Holy Spirit."

These to me are among the most significant words of the twentieth century with far-reaching consequences for the church and the world. From them flowed a renewed appreciation of the community model of church, or the church as communion, in the image of the Father, Son and Holy Spirit. When teased out, this understanding encompasses and makes real the vision of Vatican II. To be called upon in the church to be a community like the Trinity raises intriguing questions as to what kind of community the Trinity is. To choose just a few challenging facts, the Trinity is a community where there is:

- Intimate loving and sharing,
- Full participation of the three members,
- Absolute equality of persons, and
- Outreach to the other.

How do we replicate this in the church? How do we so order it that there is intimate loving and sharing, full and responsible participation of all the members of our communities and parishes, even in decision-making? How do we foster the understanding that all are fundamentally equal through their common humanity and the sacrament of baptism? And how can we make all church members appreciate that they are, as Paul puts it, a priestly people – all sharing in the priesthood of Christ and not leaving it to the ordained minister, who is chosen for certain functions? Does not the presiding minister say, after the offertory, 'Pray, sisters and brothers, that *our* sacrifice may be acceptable to God, the Father Almighty'? No claim to a monopoly there.

Well, one important way in which the major insight of Vatican Council II is being realised is *through small Christian communities that are open to, and network with, one another thereby helping to make bigger entities, such as the parish or mission station, a communion of communities.* This even though some members of the larger entities may, by choice, have only a loose connection with the communities. The example of small communities can touch the lives of all. And this, I believe, is what the church of the future should and will look like.

The future of our past

As we increasingly adopt this community-type church in the future, we will see that it is a case of going back to the future, because that is how we were at the beginning. When the disciples of Jesus came to give practical expression to his message of love in the years following his death and resurrection, small Christian communities sprang up in neighbourhoods – communities that were 'united heart and soul' (Acts 4:32). So there were the house churches, yet there was also the compulsion to come together in larger assemblies, thus forming the communion of communities. For a full experience of church, then, there seems to have been two concerns: firstly to be part of a small intimate community (cf Acts 12:12; Romans 16:5, 16:11, 16:14-15); and secondly there was the further concern to network (cf Acts 2:46; 3:11; 14:26-27). The point that stands out, however, is that the early church was, above all, communitarian. The focus was on persons rather than on institutions. We need structures; otherwise our relational projects can run into the sand. But the structures are there to foster community;

they are secondary and must never become an end in themselves.

I have a Scottish friend who believes that we need institutions but that they are only a means to more important ends. During the war it seems women took the place of men to operate buses in Glasgow and also inherited their uniforms. He was intrigued by what the women did with those formal caps: they knocked them about a bit, wore them at a jaunty angle and stuck flowers in them. This did wonders for their headgear! And this too is what we should do with institutions – knock them about a bit and stick flowers in them. It prevents them from taking themselves too seriously.

But let us get back to the subject of the small Christian communities that were foundational to the early church, are a growing phenomenon in our own day and seem likely to be a large part of our future. There are a couple of further points worth making about them.

Through the unity of their members, they make the unity of the three divine persons present in the world. They are sacraments of the Trinity, that is, they make present something we can see (a Christian community) which represents a reality we can't see (the community of the Trinity). This offers huge witness and is a tremendous privilege. It also makes real Origen's claim: 'The person who is in the church, which is full of the Holy Trinity, inhabits the universe' (Origen, *Selecta*, Ps 33, Section 1).

Another salient point is that the small Christian communities do not see themselves simply as helpful groups in the church – there's quite a sociological difference between a group and a community.[2] The most profound difference is that one joins a community to deepen relationships, whereas one goes to a group primarily for a purpose, such as, to study the Bible, learn how to pray, or save the whales.

The small Christian community is also *church* and not merely a helpful adjunct to it. It's of the essence. Even one small Christian community can say of itself that it is fully church: the local and the universal churches interpenetrate; we find the universal in the local and the local in the universal. The essential ingredients are the same: faith in Christ, love, commitment, mission and so forth. I once found small Christian communities in Africa having a celebration and wearing t-shirts with

2. James O'Halloran, *Small Christian Communities: Vision and Practicalities*, Dublin: The Columba Press, 2002, pp 77-78.

the words 'We are church'. The theology here is sound. To quote Tertullian: 'Where there are three, a church exists, although they be laity' (*Exhortation to Chastity*, 7.3).

The Kingdom of God

So far, in our projections for the future, we have been dealing with in-house matters, focusing on our church. One thing John XXIII did in convening Vatican II was to throw the windows of the church wide open, allowing fresh air to rush in after more than 400 years of stuffiness. In doing so, he pointed to the great world out there (the cosmic dimension of which Origen speaks) that needed our attention and concern, and that cried out for the promotion of God's kingdom in our midst. John was a great visionary. At first, many looked patronisingly on this old man, expecting him to serve as a benign stop-gap for a few years. He was of peasant stock, so they may even have eyed his boots for traces of cow manure. But what a surprise they got! He started a profound consideration of the kingdom and what it meant. It was this reality that forced me to change the title of this presentation from 'The Church of the Future' to 'The Church and World of the Future'.

The most important thing for Jesus in his ministry was the kingdom of God and its justice (cf Matthew 6:33). The word 'church' is used only three times in the gospel (cf Matthew 16:18; 18:17) while Christ speaks frequently of the kingdom. According to Paul VI it is 'the absolute good' to which everything else must defer (*The Evangelisation of Peoples*, no 8). Clearly, as for Christ, the kingdom has to be the priority for us. But in what does it consist?

The kingdom cannot be defined for it is a mystery. We could volunteer the following in an attempt to describe it:

• A new creation (Galatians 6:15; Revelations 21:1);

• The priority (Matthew 6:33; Luke 12:31);

• God's rule prevailing in the world (Psalm 103: 19);

• The person of Jesus: his mind, heart and values (cf Matthew 16:28; 19:29; Mark 9:1; Luke 9:27, seen widely in the 'I am' statements of John's gospel);

• Wherever there is harmony rooted in justice (Matthew 6:33; Luke12:31);

• All that is good, gracious and therefore, God revealing – where 'the blind see', 'the lame walk' (Luke 7:21), and where 'I was hungry and you fed me, thirsty and you gave me a drink' (Matthew: 25-35);

• Openness and tolerance (Matthew 20:1-16; Acts 5:34-39);

• Present and yet to come (1 Corinthians 15:12-28).

Harmony would be an abiding feature of God's kingdom, though in it we find some strange bedfellows indeed, as the beautiful images of the prophet Isaiah suggest:

The wolf shall live with the lamb,

the leopard shall lie down with the kid,

the calf, the lion, and the fatling together,

and a little child shall lead them. (Isaiah 16)

Note the highlighting of harmony; again there is the implication of community. The kingdom is a matter of unity rooted in justice. It is wherever there is goodness, and it matters not whether the goodness is found among Muslims, Hindus, Buddhists, Jews or people who would profess no religion – we will support it as a priority. One area in which people of different denominations and religions already work together is on development projects. This is fitting because there are, for example, no Catholic, Protestant, or Muslim bridges. Bridges are ecumenical and permit everyone, whatever

their persuasion, to get over a river in safety.
This opens up a world vista for us beyond our
particular persuasion. Our first concern must
be to work for a better world for everyone, and
we are not simply talking about the hereafter,
but also of the here and now. We aspire to noth-
ing less than a new heaven and a new earth
(Revelations 1:1).

In what I have been saying regarding the
kingdom as the priority, there is no thought of
diminishing the church or downplaying the
role of Christ. We believe Jesus is the Saviour of
all, and church members are parts of his body.
The church is not the whole of the kingdom, as
we have seen – it is part of it. But surely it is
meant to be a powerful example of it and an
effective instrument for building it on the planet.
Furthermore, what better way to attract people
to Christ and the Christian community than to
have a church that promotes the kingdom in
the world?

In building this kingdom, or a better world,
openness and tolerance are important. I have to
say that in my work worldwide I continually
found myself challenged by the Spirit to openness. This often caused pain because we all
have constraints depending on the time and
place in which we live. Even Jesus had con-

straints. One such was that he was sent to minister to the lost sheep of the house of Israel only (Matthew 15:24) and was put in a quandary when Gentiles sought his intervention. Yet the interesting thing is that he always responded to faith; we saw him do it with the Roman centurion (Matthew 8:5-13) and the Canaanite woman (Matthew 15:21-28). I daresay Jesus came to ask himself how he could possibly refuse healing to people who so obviously had faith. Despite our constraints, if we maintain open minds and do our best, God's purposes will be achieved. In the context of openness, I believe that Pope Benedict XVI's recent visit (2006) to Turkey and outreach to the Muslim community have done immense good.

Justice

Justice is to the kingdom what oxygen is to life. They have to go together. Jesus does not say merely, 'Seek first the kingdom,' but adds significantly, 'and its justice …' (Matthew 6:33); we cannot have the harmony without the justice.

Justice, according to the Bible and the documents of the church, means having right relationships with:

- Self,
- God,

- Neighbour, and
- Environment.

Oftentimes when we speak of justice, we are thinking of economic justice: fair returns for our work, proper conditions in industrial plants and so on. Justice, however, is much more than that because it touches all aspects of our lives. It is total in its approach to relationships and unity. I will neither wantonly hurt a neighbour, nor needlessly set foot upon a worm.

I once heard a woman of African origin say at a meeting in a São Paulo *favela*, or deprived district: 'I am oppressed three times over. I'm oppressed because I am poor; I'm oppressed because I am black; and I'm oppressed because I am a woman.' I was somewhat surprised to hear her say, for example, that she was oppressed because she was a woman. The men in the district, after all, were passionately involved in issues of justice. And yet this woman, and others as it turned out, felt downtrodden because of their gender. So, apparently, the menfolk still lacked a clear understanding of the full nature of justice. We all have our blindspots.

Small Christian Communities and Vatican II

The point was made earlier that the communities gave flesh and blood to the vision of Vatican Council II. The elements of that vision, due in no small part to the inspiration of John XXIII, were overwhelmingly approved by the 2,540 bishops in St Peter's Basilica. This was the greatest event in 600 years of the church's history. The greatest act of discernment for centuries. It aroused enormous popular interest and support[3] and was all that the pope and the assembled fathers prayed for: 'the inauguration of a new era'… 'a flash of sublime illumination'… 'a new Pentecost'.[4]

The elements of the vision that point to the church and world of the future are as follows:

- A warm (pastoral) style of operation instead of a rigid insistence on rules and regulations;
- A following of the spirit rather than the letter of the law;
- Evangelisation, above all, a matter of sharing the good news of Jesus Christ;
- An ecumenical openness to other

3. Alberigo, Guiseppe, *A Brief History of Vatican II,* New York: Orbis Books, 2006, p 130.
4. Ibid, p 119.

Christian denominations and other religions;

• An increase in authority for local churches (dioceses, parishes and small communities) to run their own affairs in accordance with the principles of subsidiarity and decentralisation;

• Decision-making through dialogue and consensus;

• Leadership understood as service, not domination;

• Giving due clout to the laity – God's priestly people;

• The ever-increasing importance of women;

• A growing appreciation of God's word being at the heart of all our projects;

• Guidelines to be decided in accordance with a warm pastoral approach, consideration of what is happening in the world around us and a desire for peace;

• Guidelines always inspired by a profound trust in the Holy Spirit, in the inherent faith of the people and their ability to be creative and imaginative;

• Promotion of equality, simplicity of life, justice, peace and Christian unity;

• A Christ-like choice (option) on behalf of the poor and oppressed;

- Respect for history and historical setting, bearing in mind that God is always active in history; indeed, through Jesus, God became one of us – Emmanuel or God with us;
- Teaching that arises from life experience and is not airily divorced from our daily struggles;
- The fostering of a community model of church that, above all, furthers the kingdom of God and its justice and reaches out to all the peoples of the world (as already noticed, this item encompasses and could serve as a summary of the foregoing points).[5]

This was the council's vision. And Pope John gave a practical orientation for implementing it, noting that it was necessary to distinguish between the substance of ancient doctrine and the means of presenting it. The truths underlying the great mysteries of Christianity (the incarnation, the cross, resurrection, Trinity and so on) never change. What does and should change is the language we use to express them, which should use words and ideas of our particular time. The world moves on. We never stand in the same river twice.

5. Alberigo, Guiseppe and Komanchak Joseph eds., *History of Vatican II*, New York: Orbis Books, 2006. Confer to substantiate vision.

Implementation

By now you may be wondering what became of this wonderful vision and methodology. To borrow from quite another source, they haven't gone away you know. But sadly we would have to say that much remains to be done. During the council special commissions were set up to deal with specific areas (the church, liturgy, revelation and so forth) and these proved quite efficient. Yet once the council finished, the task of implementing it was left to the Roman Curia, which probably had enough to do besides that. Furthermore, the Curia was the body that showed least enthusiasm for the council; indeed the Curia's schemes for conducting it were dropped early on.

The triennial Synod of Bishops, established in the wake of the council to assist the pope with governing the church, never got the clout it needed for the task. So decentralisation, subsidiarity and collegiality – great aims of Vatican II – languished. Happily, they now seem to be staging a comeback. The situation was not helped either by the worldwide student uprisings of 1968. Many felt that authority itself was under threat and lost their nerve for renewal. A pity because the baby got thrown out with the bath water.[6]

At this point, some small Christian communities, particularly in Europe, decided there could be no going back on the gains of Vatican II and continued to take the vision forward. Indeed, the same would be true of small communities throughout the world. They do not see themselves, nor do they want to be, an alternative or parallel church. But they do see themselves as a new way of being church in accordance with the vision of Vatican II.

Having worked with the communities now for thirty-six years, I too see them as that. They are a practical working out of paragraph 4 in the *Dogmatic Constitution on the Church* which says that we should be a community in the image of the Trinity.

Indeed, bearing in mind the primacy of the kingdom of God, I would now state my own position as a matter of: *promoting small Christian communities and encouraging them to form communions of communities, but I would foster groups of all kinds, whether religious or civic, that are doing anything to build a better world. And I would*

6. Cf Ian M. Fraser, *Living a Countersign: From Iona to Basic Christian Communities,* Glasgow: Wild Goose Publications, 1990, p 14.

have them link up with and support one another in their endeavours. This too involves not only a vision, but also a practical orientation for implementing it.

Spirituality of community

Spirituality might be defined as a lived experience of faith, and people who have reflected upon their communal path have come up with a spirituality that they will no doubt go on refining into the future.

Christopher Mwoleka is a community member whom I must name. He is now deceased, but I found he gave me profound inspiration. Mwoleka looked at his small Christian community in Tanzania and said: 'We are a dozen [or whatever] distinct and estimable persons here, yet through our intimate loving and sharing we are one. We are like the Trinity: three persons but one God, or one community.' This is a straightforward insight. Nevertheless, as we have already seen, it has tremendous consequences. *The consciousness of small Christian communities being rooted in the Trinity would be the most important feature of their spirituality.*

Following from this is the role of the Son, Jesus, whose body the church is (true) but who is also seen as the dearest of friends. Members are also ever conscious of the presence of the Spirit whose guidance is sought at all times.

Mwoleka, incidentally, was a bishop who lived in an Ujamaa village in the same conditions as other villagers – no palace for him, no dreaming spires. Ujamaa ('togetherness') villages were promoted by the outstanding President Julius Nyrere of Tanzania as places where people could live and farm together in community. They were also a means of gathering people in convenient centres where services such as health and education could more easily be provided. If people were thinly scattered, this task would be made more difficult.

Moleka believed this to be a worthy scheme, so he himself lived and farmed in such a village. In the evenings, he would sit and chat and smoke his pipe with other farmers and other community members. Regarding his insight that small Christian communities are rooted in the unity of the Father, Son, and Holy Spirit, I have found no one who would disagree. As Tanzanian Christians aptly put it: 'There are three dancers, but only one dance.'

Being rooted in the Trinity gives Christians

a profound sense of being permeated by the love of God, God who is love (1 John 4:8). We belong to God. God holds us in the palm of his hand. Even before we were born or could begin to love, God first loved us (cf John 15:12). And this love of God is without conditions. The Lord doesn't say: 'I will love you but only if you are good.' Whether we are good or bad, God still loves us and works for our salvation. God is love and cannot do otherwise. God's love for us is something that we have to know, not just in the head but in the heart or, more graphically, in the gut.

When people are conscious of this love, it can change the whole way in which they see life. Take human love. They know that, when they give a neighbour an experience of genuine love, they are giving them an experience of God, because God is love – the source. So our human love is the channelling of the love of God to one another. If this is not what happens when I love Mary or Tom, then that love is not true. But if I channel God's love to others, then I will always love sensitively and well. The poet William Blake puts it so tellingly, when he says that we are: 'put on earth that we may learn to bear the beams of love'.

Issuing from the fact that community finds

its inspiration in the community of Father, Son
and Spirit, the members stress the following
items:

- Faith enhancing life and leading to action;
- A strong prayerful dimension embracing
the word of God, prayer, the eucharist,
reflection and reconciliation;
- An emergence of 'the new person' men-
tioned in Ephesians 4:24;
- Sensitivity towards, and respect for, local
cultures;
- The kingdom and its justice as a priority;
- Openness to those different from ourselves;
- A spirit of perseverance;
- A resistance towards the showy and flam-
boyant;
- A hunger for knowledge of God;
- A joyful spirit.

Laughter and the love of friends
The spirituality of community might be graphically stated as *befriending one another in God,
Three in One.* It's about intimacy. That love and
relationships are of the essence has sometimes
been expressed more vitally by secular rather
than by spiritual authors (Blake, already quoted,
was a mystic and would, I believe, have to be
ranked among spiritual scribes). Hilaire Belloc,

undoubtedly catholic yet secular, is uncannily
accurate when he writes:

> From quiet homes and first beginning,
> Out to the undiscovered ends,
> There's nothing worth the wear of winning,
> But laughter and the love of friends.
> *(Dedicatory Ode)*

Raymond Carver, too, while dying young after
a difficult life – a life in which he nevertheless
experienced love at the end – penned these
poignant lines:

> And did you get what
> You wanted from life even so?
> I did.
> And what did you want?
> To call myself beloved, to feel myself
> Beloved on the earth.
> *(Last Fragment)*

Only if we have loved, have we truly lived.
'Laughter and the love of friends' ... 'to feel
myself beloved'... 'tasting the sweetness of
togetherness' – these are the seeming trivia of
every day life. Only they are not trivia. They
are an expression of "the burthen of the mystery". Their origins are found within the fath-
omless depths of the Blessed Trinity. But wasn't

it all summarised by the Man himself long ago:
'Love one another as I have loved you.'

c.c.or.

Select Bibliography

Alberigo, Guiseppe, *A Brief History of Vatican II*, New York: Orbis Books, 2006. An excellent synthesis.

Alberigo, Guiseppe and Komanchak, Joseph, eds., *History of Vatican II,* five volumes, New York: Orbis Books, 1995-2006. The definitive history of Vatican II.

Fraser, Ian M., *Many Cells One Body: Stories from Small Christian Communities,* Geneva: World Council of Churches Publications, 2003. This book marvellously reflects a lifetime of interaction and correspondence with small Christian communities.

Healey, Joseph G., and Hinton Jeanne, eds., *Small Christian Communities Today: Capturing the New Moment,* New York: Orbis Books, 2005. 'Displays the gems that come from pastoral experience where parishes are renewed as communities of many small communities.' *RENEW International*

Madges, William, ed., *Vatican II: Forty Years Later*, New York: Orbis Books, 2006. Superb and insightful essays.

O'Halloran, James, *Small Christian Communities: Vision and Practicalities,* Dublin: The Columba Press, 2002; Chester Springs, PA: Dufour Editions, 2002. '… a vision of a renewed Church…A text of unimpeachable quality'. *Hallel*, Europe
— *In Search of Christ: A Prayer Book for Seekers*, Dublin: The Columba Press, 2004; Chester Springs, PA: Dufour Editions, 2004. 'O'Halloran's model [of lectio divina – Bible reflection] is simplicity itself'. Amazon.ca

— *Saving the Fish from Drowning: Reflections from the Barrio*, Dublin: The Columba Press, 2006; Chester Springs, PA: Dufour Editions, 2006. 'Creates a longing to begin a ministry of service all over again – this time more perfectly. Never a time when it is impossible to begin again.' *Books Ireland*

— *The Brendan Book of Prayer, for small groups*, Dublin: The Columba Press, 2003; Chester Springs, PA: Dufour Editions, 2003. 'O'Halloran's model [of lectio divina – Bible reflection] is simplicity itself.' Amazon.ca

Rynne, Xavier, *Vatican Council II*, New York: Orbis Books, 1999. 'The best account of what the Council is all about'. *New York Times*

Books relevant to Callan
Kennedy, Joseph ed. (advised by Seamus O'Brien), *Dawn on the Irish Coast, Poems by John Locke*, Kilkenny: Boethius Press, 2nd edition, 1985. 'The Poet of Ireland-in-Exile.'

Callan, County Kilkenny (Text: Joseph Kennedy; Sketches: Tara Delaney; Photos: Philip Lynch), Callan Heritage Society, 2nd edition, 2000.

Fitzgerald, John, *Callan in the Rare Old Times*, Kilkenny: Callan Press, 2003.
— *Callan through the Mists of Time*, Kilkenny: Callan Press, 2004.

By the same author

When the Acacia Bird Sings
A NOVEL

'A must for anyone who wishes to understand the pain of separation suffered by migrants and refugees. If ever a book should be on the national curriculum, this is it.'
– Tom Hyland, 'Books of the Year', The Irish Times

'A novel of stature. I read it at a sitting, not because of its brevity – rather the story of the Machava family had gripped me intensely. Its humane perceptions remind me of Andre Brink's celebrated books. Brings the open minded reader to where literature raises timely moral questions.'
– Denis Carroll, The Furrow

'This is a harrowing narrative and an epic in the classic sense, spare and stark in its prose style. There are echoes of Antigone trying to bury her dead. Very well written.'
– Rita Kelly, Books Ireland

'Having read *Remember José Inga!* by the same author, I was so impressed that I asked to see this book. O'Halloran tells a truth we need to know.'
– Mary Bartholomew, GoodBookSTall and BBC Cumbria, England

By the same author

Remember José Inga!
A NOVEL

'A good novel. Yes! But so much more. Having read it, I was so impressed that I asked to see *When the Acacia Bird Sings* by the same author. O'Halloran's experience gives the story a feeling of accurate history, and arouses our emotions.

– *Mary Bartholomew, GoodBookStall and BBC Cumbria, England*

'This novel describes graphically the sometimes brutal forces that keep people in poverty and the gigantic struggle it is for those who are oppressed to change their situation ... The general reader will find *Remember José Inga!* deeply engaging and it will be of particular interest to people committed to peace and justice, who will find this book hugely informative and inspiring.'

– *Shay Claffey, St Anthony's Messenger, Ireland*

By the same author

The Least of These
A selection of short stories

'O'Halloran writes with a shrewd eye and accurate ear, catching and holding the reader's attention with some startlingly precise images and with dialogue so natural and accurate the reader feels at times as if he were eavesdropping on the characters of these tales … a skilled collection by a gifted writer.'
– *Brendan Kennelly, Trinity College, Dublin*

'Highlights a variety of issues at the core of justice and peace in an easy, attractive way that immediately engages the sympathy of the reader … the language is simple and beautiful, the stories very moving … The volume is warm and human, based on a life at the front line.'
— *Alo Donnelly, former Executive Director, Concern Universal, England*

All the foregoing available at:

• Australia: Rainbow Books, 303 Arthur Street, Fairfield, Vic 3078, T. 03 9481 6611, Email: rba@rainbooks.com.au

• Canada: Anglican Book Centre, 80 Hayden Street, Toronto, ON M4Y 3G2, T. 1800 268 1168, Email abc@anglicanbookcentre.com
Bayard Distribution, 49 Front Street East, Toronto, ON M5E 1B3, T. 416 363 3303 Email: tradebooks@bayard-inc.com

• Ireland: The Columba Press, 55A Spruce Avenue, Stillorgan Industrial Park, Blackrock, Co Dublin, T. +353 (0)1 2942556 Email: sales@columba.ie
little book company, 11 Hillsbrook Crescent, Perrystown, Dublin 12, T. (01) 4555453 Email: dbmullan@eircom.net

• Europe: Durnell Marketing Ltd, 2 Linden Close, Tunbridge Wells, Kent TN4, 8HH, UK, T. 44 1892 544 272, Email: mail@durnell.co.uk

• New Zealand: Pleroma, 38 Higginson St, Otane 4170, Central Hawkes Bay, New Zealand. T. 06 856 8378, Email: management@pleroma.org.nz

• USA: Dufour Editions, PO Box 7, Chester Springs, PA 19425-0007, T. 1800 869 5677 or 610 458 5005, Email: info@dufoureditions.com